11+ STYLE TEST PAPERS
ENGLISH

THE S6 TUTORING ACADEMY

11⁺ STYLE TEST PAPERS

ENGLISH

THE S6 TUTORING ACADEMY

5 PRACTICE TESTS WITH COMPLETE ANSWERS

TOPICS INCLUDE: READING COMPREHENSION, APPLIED REASONING AND ADVANCED GRAMMAR

Matador
9 Priory Business Park,
Wistow Road, Kibworth Beauchamp,
Leicestershire. LE8 0RX
Tel: (+44) 116 279 2299
Fax: (+44) 116 279 2277
Email: books@troubador.co.uk
Web: www.troubador.co.uk/matador

ISBN 978 1784623 210

British Library Cataloguing in Publication Data.
A catalogue record for this book is available from the British Library.

Typeset in Bell Gothic by Troubador Publishing Ltd, Leicester, UK

Matador is an imprint of Troubador Publishing Ltd

All who have accomplished great things have had a great aim, have fixed their gaze on a goal which was high, one which sometimes seemed impossible. Thus, aim high in your career but stay humble in your heart.

Contents

English Mock Exam
Paper 1

Please Complete Your Details:

Name. ....

School: ....

Boy or Girl: ....

Date of Birth: ....

Today's Date: ....

Please Complete Your Details:

Name ....

School ....

Boy or Girl ....

Date of Birth ....

Today's Date ....

Read the following instructions carefully:

1. Do not open or turn over this page until you have been instructed to do so.

2. Read the text carefully when you are told to do so and then complete the questions that follow.

3. Work as quickly and as carefully as you can.

4. Write your answer to the question ONLY in the space provided.

5. If you want to change your answer, either rub out your original answer or put a single line through it and then write the new answer.

6. If you cannot answer a question, go on to the next question.

7. The number of marks available for each question is indicated in the right-hand margin.

8. Punctuation should be both clear and exact.

9. Where you are asked to choose between a number of possible responses, always choose the **most appropriate** response.

10. You will have **10 minutes** reading time before starting the test.

11. You will have **60 minutes** in total to complete the test.

12. Once the test has begun, you should not ask about questions in the test.

13. When you have completed this practice paper go back to any questions you have missed out and check all of your answers.

English Mock Exam Paper 1

10 minutes reading time
60 minutes to complete the test

Suggested timing for candidates:

Reading time	10 minutes
Section One – Comprehension	30 minutes
Section Two – Applied Reasoning	10 minutes
Section Three – Continuous Writing	20 minutes

When you are told to do so, carefully read the passage on the next page. After 10 minutes has ended you will have 60 minutes to complete the test. Answer the questions which are on the following pages.

The following passage is from *20,000 Leagues Under the Sea* by Jules Verne

1 The narwhal seemed motionless; perhaps, tired with its day's work, it slept, letting itself float with
2 the undulation of the waves. Now was a chance of which the captain resolved to take advantage.
3 He gave his orders. The Abraham Lincoln kept up half steam, and advanced cautiously so as not to
4 awake its adversary. It is no rare thing to meet in the middle of the ocean whales so sound asleep
5 that they can be successfully attacked, and Ned Land had harpooned more than one during its sleep.
6 The Canadian went to take his place again under the bowsprit.
7 The frigate approached noiselessly, stopped at two cables' lengths from the animal, and following its
8 track. No one breathed; a deep silence reigned on the bridge. We were not a hundred feet from the
9 burning focus, the light of which increased and dazzled our eyes.
10 At this moment, leaning on the forecastle bulwark, I saw below me Ned Land grappling the
11 martingale in one hand, brandishing his terrible harpoon in the other, scarcely twenty feet from the
12 motionless animal. Suddenly his arm straightened, and the harpoon was thrown; I heard the
13 sonorous stroke of the weapon, which seemed to have struck a hard body. The electric light went
14 out suddenly, and two enormous waterspouts broke over the bridge of the frigate, rushing like a
15 torrent from stem to stern, overthrowing men, and breaking the lashings of the spars. A fearful
16 shock followed, and, thrown over the rail without having time to stop myself, I fell into the sea.
17 This unexpected fall so stunned me that I have no clear recollection of my sensations at the time. I
18 was at first drawn down to a depth of about twenty feet. I am a good swimmer (though without
19 pretending to rival Byron or Edgar Poe, who were masters of the art), and in that plunge I did not
20 lose my presence of mind. Two vigorous strokes brought me to the surface of the water. My first
21 care was to look for the frigate. Had the crew seen me disappear? Had the Abraham Lincoln veered
22 round? Would the captain put out a boat? Might I hope to be saved?
23 The darkness was intense. I caught a glimpse of a black mass disappearing in the east, its beacon
24 lights dying out in the distance. It was the frigate! I was lost.
25 "Help, help!" I shouted, swimming towards the Abraham Lincoln in desperation.
26 My clothes encumbered me; they seemed glued to my body, and paralysed my movements.
27 I was sinking! I was suffocating!
28 "Help!"
29 This was my last cry. My mouth filled with water; I struggled against being drawn down the abyss.
30 Suddenly my clothes were seized by a strong hand, and I felt myself quickly drawn up to the surface
31 of the sea; and I heard, yes, I heard these words pronounced in my ear:
32 "If master would be so good as to lean on my shoulder, master would swim with much greater
33 ease."
34 I seized with one hand my faithful Conseil's arm.
35 "Is it you?" said I, "you?"
36 "Myself," answered Conseil; "and waiting Master's orders."
37 "That shock threw you as well as me into the sea?"
38 "No; but, being in my master's service, I followed him."
39 The worthy fellow thought that was but natural.
40 "And the frigate?" I asked.
41 "The frigate?" replied Conseil, turning on his back; "I think that Master had better not count too
42 much on her."
43 "You think so?"

44 "I say that, at the time I threw myself into the sea, I heard the men at the wheel say, `The screw and
45 the rudder are broken.'
46 "Broken?"
47 "Yes, broken by the monster's teeth. It is the only injury the Abraham Lincoln has sustained. But it is
48 a bad look-out for us—she no longer answers her helm."
49 "Then we are lost!"
50 "Perhaps so," calmly answered Conseil. "However, we have still several hours before us, and one can
51 do a good deal in some hours."
52 Conseil's imperturbable coolness set me up again. I swam more vigorously; but, cramped by my
53 clothes, which stuck to me like a leaden weight, I felt great difficulty in bearing up. Conseil saw this.
54 "Will Master let me make a slit?" said he; and, slipping an open knife under my clothes, he ripped
55 them up from top to bottom very rapidly. Then he cleverly slipped them off me, while I swam for
56 both of us.
57 Then I did the same for Conseil, and we continued to swim near to each other.
58 Nevertheless, our situation was no less terrible. Perhaps our disappearance had not been noticed;
59 and, if it had been, the frigate could not tack, being without its helm. Conseil argued on this
60 supposition, and laid his plans accordingly. This quiet boy was perfectly self-possessed. We then
61 decided that, as our only chance of safety was being picked up by the Abraham Lincoln's boats, we
62 ought to manage so as to wait for them as long as possible. I resolved then to husband our strength,
63 so that both should not be exhausted at the same time; and this is how we managed: while one of us
64 lay on our back, quite still, with arms crossed, and legs stretched out, the other would swim and
65 push the other on in front. This towing business did not last more than ten minutes each; and
66 relieving each other thus, we could swim on for some hours, perhaps till daybreak. Poor chance! but
67 hope is so firmly rooted in the heart of man! Moreover, there were two of us. Indeed I declare
68 (though it may seem improbable) if I sought to destroy all hope—if I wished to despair, I could not.
69 The collision of the frigate with the cetacean had occurred about eleven o'clock in the evening
70 before. I reckoned then we should have eight hours to swim before sunrise, an operation quite
71 practicable if we relieved each other. The sea, very calm, was in our favour. Sometimes I tried to
72 pierce the intense darkness that was only dispelled by the phosphorescence caused by our
73 movements. I watched the luminous waves that broke over my hand, whose mirror-like surface was
74 spotted with silvery rings. One might have said that we were in a bath of quicksilver.
75 Near one o'clock in the morning, I was seized with dreadful fatigue. My limbs stiffened under the
76 strain of violent cramp. Conseil was obliged to keep me up, and our preservation devolved on him
77 alone. I heard the poor boy pant; his breathing became short and hurried. I found that he could not
78 keep up much longer.
79 "Leave me! Leave me!" I said to him.
80 "Leave my master? Never!" replied he. "I would drown first."

Section One – Comprehension

Spend about 30 minutes on this section

1. What is the Abraham Lincoln? (Tick **ONE** box) A. A whale .... ☐ B. A frigate .... ☐ C. A poet .... ☐ D. The captain's adversary .... ☐	1 mark
2. Which of the following statements is not true when considering the first part of this passage? Lines 1 – 9 (Tick **ONE** box) A. The ship is travelling slowly .... ☐ B. The Canadian has done this before .... ☐ C. The whale is asleep .... ☐ D. The sea is iced over .... ☐	1 mark
3. Which of the following best describes the emotions of the men on the boat from lines 1 – 9? (Tick **THREE** boxes) A. Apprehensive .... ☐ B. In awe .... ☐ C. Fearful .... ☐ D. Reassured .... ☐ E. Devoted .... ☐ F. Anxious .... ☐	3 marks
4. Which four words suggest frenzied action in lines 10 – 16? (Tick **FOUR** boxes) A. Brandishing.. ☐ B. Terrible.. ☐ C. Suddenly.. ☐ D. Rushing.. ☐ E. Fearful... ☐ F. Torrent.. ☐ G. Overthrowing.. ☐	4 marks

11

5. (a) In lines 13 – 16 find a SIMILE. Write out the simile. .... (b) Explain the meaning of this simile.	1 mark 2 marks
6. Look at lines 21 – 22. Which of the following best describes the emotions of the narrator? (Tick **ONE** box) A. Confused .... ☐ B. Panicked .... ☐ C. Jubilant .... ☐ D. Apprehensive .... ☐	1 mark
7. What signs are there that the narrator is feeling terror in lines 23 – 31? (Tick **THREE** boxes) A. He uses exclamations to show the ship leaving .... ☐ B. He begins to tread water .... ☐ C. He shouts with extreme anxiety .... ☐ D. His eyes cloud over with tears .... ☐ E. He believes he is falling underwater, to be lost forever .... ☐ F. He flails his arms around .... ☐	3 marks
8. Which THREE of these details are true from lines 23 – 51? (Tick **THREE** boxes) A. The ship is coming back to get him................................. ☐ B. The ship heard the man's cries....................................... ☐ C. The narrator has difficulty moving because of his clothes...... ☐ D. The ship is catastrophically damaged.............................. ☐ E. The narrator's servant saves him.................................... ☐ F. The rough sea has broken the boat.................................. ☐	3 marks

9. Which two words/phrases from lines 32 – 40 suggest that Conseil is a good man? (Tick **TWO** boxes) A. Master's service.. ☐ B. Worthy fellow.. ☐ C. Natural.. ☐ D. Faithful .... ☐	2 marks
10. Which of the following best describes the reactions the narrator or Conseil have to their situation from lines 50 to the end of the passage? (Tick **TWO** boxes) A. Contented.. ☐ B. Absurd... ☐ C. Composed.. ☐ D. Fatigued.. ☐ E. Indolent.. ☐ F. Spirited.. ☐	2 marks
11. Why is Conseil described as 'self-possessed'?	1 mark
12. Select from the passage one word which most closely corresponds to the word or phrase on the left. The right-hand column below provides guidance regarding which lines to look at to find the correct word.	12 marks

	Word from passage	Look in lines
A. Stationary	....	1 – 3
B. Ripple	....	2 – 4
C. Foe	....	3 – 6
D. Governed	....	7 – 10
E. Resonant	....	10 – 15
F. Reminiscence	....	15 – 20
G. Strong	....	20 – 25
H. Impeded	....	25 – 30

I. Incurred	....	45 – 50	12 marks
J. Belief	....	60 – 65	
K. Strived	....	65 – 70	
L. Transferred	....	75 – 80	

13. In one sentence explain what the narrator's plan is to keep them alive. | 1 mark

....

....

14. (a) Look at lines 70 – 75, write down the metaphor that is written there. | 1 mark

....

(b) Explain what the metaphor means. | 2 marks

....

....

Section Two – Applied Reasoning

Spend about 10 minutes on this section

Complete the words using the **same** letter in each gap. *Example:* ha(_)d (_)obot *should be completed* ha(r)d (r)obot ra(_)(_)le dra(_)t *should be completed* ra(f)(f)le dra(f)t	
Question 1 co(_)nt f(_)nd	1 mark
Question 2 gri(_)v(_) d(_)lud(_)	1 mark
Complete the words using the **same** letter to end the first word and start the second. *Example:* rada(_)obot *should be completed* rada(r)obot baske(_)able *should be completed* baske(t)able	
Question 3 preac(_)aste	1 mark
Question 4 pas(_)olve	1 mark
Question 5 Shorter words can be made by rearranging the letters of the word **mustard** For example: the word **star** can be made with four of the letters. **Find five other four-letter words that can be made from 'mustard'.** 1. .... 2. .... 3. .... 4. .... 5.	1 mark

Section Three – Continuous Writing

Spend about 20 minutes on these 2 questions

1. Write five or six sentences describing your house. Make your writing as vivid as possible.	15 marks

....

....

....

....

....

....

....

....

....

....

2. In five or six sentences, write clear instructions on how to boil an egg. Make your writing as precise as possible.

....

....

....

....

....

....

....

....

....

End of Test

End of Test

English Mock Exam Paper 1
ANSWERS

Question	Answer	Mark
1.	B	1
2.	D	1
3.	A B F	3
4.	C D F G	4
5.	(a) rushing like a torrent *from stem to stern* (italics not necessary to get mark) (b) It shows how quickly and forcefully the water is moving over the boat. *Or similar answer.*	1 1 for idea of speed, 1 for Idea of force
6.	B	1
7.	A C E	3
8.	C D E	3
9.	B D	2
10.	C D	2
11.	He is described as self-possessed because he is able to think of a plan whilst under pressure/he doesn't panic. *Or similar answer.*	1
12.	A. Motionless	1
	B. Undulation	1
	C. Adversary	1
	D. Reigned	1
	E. Sonorous	1
	F. Recollection	1
	G. Intense	1
	H. Encumbered	1
	I. Sustained	1
	J. Supposition	1
	K. Sought	1
	L. Devolved	1

13.	Only one will swim at a time while the other floats, then they will swap places. *Or similar answer, must be in a complete sentence.*	1
14.	(a) we were in a bath of quicksilver	1
	(b) It shows how shiny and metallic the water looked, just like mercury	1 for idea of shiny, 1 for idea of mercury
Applied Reasoning: Q1: u Q2: e Q3: h Q4: s Q5: must, drat, rams, tars, drum, rats, stud – there are more, mark any real word as correct (1 mark for each question)		5 marks
Continuous Writing: This will be marked as one piece of work and the candidate will be assessed on accuracy, spelling, punctuation, the quality of writing and originality.		15 marks
	Total	60 marks

English Mock Exam
Paper 2

Please Complete Your Details:

Name: ....

School: ....

Boy or Girl: ....

Date of Birth: ....

Today's Date: ....

Please Complete Your Details:

Name: ....

School: ....

Boy or Girl: ....

Date of Birth: ....

Today's Date: ....

Read the following instructions carefully:

1. Do not open or turn over this page until you have been instructed to do so.

2. Read the text carefully when you are told to do so and then complete the questions that follow.

3. Work as quickly and as carefully as you can.

4. Write your answer to the question ONLY in the space provided.

5. If you want to change your answer, either rub out your original answer or put a single line through it and then write the new answer.

6. If you cannot answer a question, go on to the next question.

7. The number of marks available for each question is indicated in the right-hand margin.

8. Punctuation should be both clear and exact.

9. Where you are asked to choose between a number of possible responses, always choose the **most appropriate** response.

10. You will have **10 minutes** reading time before starting the test.

11. You will have **60 minutes** in total to complete the test.

12. Once the test has begun, you should not ask about questions in the test.

13. When you have completed this practice paper go back to any questions you have missed out and check all of your answers.

English Mock Exam
Paper 2

10 minutes reading time

60 minutes to complete the test

Suggested timing for candidates:

Reading time	10 minutes
Section One – Comprehension	30 minutes
Section Two – Applied Reasoning	10 minutes
Section Three – Continuous Writing	20 minutes

When you are told to do so, carefully read the passage on the next page. After 10 minutes has ended you will have 60 minutes to complete the test. Answer the questions which are on the following pages.

The following passage is from *Adam Bede* by George Eliot

1 It was along the broadest of these paths that Arthur Donnithorne passed, under an avenue of limes
2 and beeches. It was a still afternoon—the golden light was lingering languidly among the upper
3 boughs, only glancing down here and there on the purple pathway and its edge of faintly sprinkled
4 moss: an afternoon in which destiny disguises her cold awful face behind a hazy radiant veil,
5 encloses us in warm downy wings, and poisons us with violet-scented breath. Arthur strolled along
6 carelessly, with a book under his arm, but not looking on the ground as meditative men are apt to
7 do; his eyes would fix themselves on the distant bend in the road round which a little figure must
8 surely appear before long. Ah! There she comes. First a bright patch of colour, like a tropic bird
9 among the boughs; then a tripping figure, with a round hat on, and a small basket under her arm;
10 then a deep-blushing, almost frightened, but bright-smiling girl, making her curtsy with a fluttered
11 yet happy glance, as Arthur came up to her. If Arthur had had time to think at all, he would have
12 thought it strange that he should feel fluttered too, be conscious of blushing too—in fact, look and
13 feel as foolish as if he had been taken by surprise instead of meeting just what he expected. Poor
14 things! It was a pity they were not in that golden age of childhood when they would have stood face
15 to face, eyeing each other with timid liking, then given each other a little butterfly kiss, and toddled
16 off to play together. Arthur would have gone home to his silk-curtained cot, and Hetty to her home-
17 spun pillow, and both would have slept without dreams, and tomorrow would have been a life
18 hardly conscious of a yesterday.
19 Arthur turned round and walked by Hetty's side without giving a reason. They were alone together
20 for the first time. What an overpowering presence that first privacy is! He actually dared not look at
21 this little butter-maker for the first minute or two. As for Hetty, her feet rested on a cloud, and she
22 was borne along by warm zephyrs; she had forgotten her rose-coloured ribbons; she was no more
23 conscious of her limbs than if her childish soul had passed into a water lily, resting on a liquid bed
24 and warmed by the midsummer sunbeams. It may seem a contradiction, but Arthur gathered a
25 certain carelessness and confidence from his timidity: it was an entirely different state of mind from
26 what he had expected in such a meeting with Hetty; and full as he was of vague feeling, there was
27 room, in those moments of silence, for the thought that his previous debates and scruples were
28 needless.
29 "You are quite right to choose this way of coming to the Chase," he said at last, looking down at
30 Hetty; "it is so much prettier as well as shorter than coming by either of the lodges."
31 "Yes, sir," Hetty answered, with a tremulous, almost whispering voice. She didn't know one bit how
32 to speak to a gentleman like Mr Arthur, and her very vanity made her more coy of speech.
33 "Do you come every week to see Mrs Pomfret?"
34 "Yes, sir, every Thursday, only when she's got to go out with Miss Donnithorne."
35 "And she's teaching you something, is she?"
36 "Yes, sir, the lace-mending as she learnt abroad, and the stocking-mending—it looks just like the
37 stocking, you can't tell it's been mended; and she teaches me cutting-out too."
38 "What! Are you going to be a lady's maid?"
39 "I should like to be one very much indeed." Hetty spoke more audibly now, but still rather
40 tremulously; she thought, perhaps she seemed as stupid to Captain Donnithorne as Luke Britton did
41 to her.
42 "I suppose Mrs Pomfret always expects you at this time?"
43 "She expects me at four o'clock. I'm rather late today, because my aunt couldn't spare me; but the

44 regular time is four, because that gives us time before Miss Donnithorne's bell rings."

45 "Ah, then, I must not keep you now, else I should like to show you the Hermitage. Did you ever see

46 it?"

47 "No, sir."

48 "This is the walk where we turn up to it. But we must not go now. I'll show it you some other time, if

49 you'd like to see it."

50 "Yes, please, sir."

51 "Do you always come back this way in the evening, or are you afraid to come so lonely a road?"

52 "Oh no, sir, it's never late; I always set out by eight o'clock, and it's so light now in the evening. My

53 aunt would be angry with me if I didn't get home before nine."

54 "Perhaps Craig, the gardener, comes to take care of you?"

55 A deep blush overspread Hetty's face and neck. "I'm sure he doesn't; I'm sure he never did; I wouldn't

56 let him; I don't like him," she said hastily, and the tears of vexation had come so fast that before she

57 had done speaking a bright drop rolled down her hot cheek. Then she felt ashamed to death that she

58 was crying, and for one long instant her happiness was all gone. But in the next she felt an arm steal

59 round her, and a gentle voice said, "Why, Hetty, what makes you cry? I didn't mean to vex you. I

60 wouldn't vex you for the world, you little blossom. Come, don't cry; look at me, else I shall think you

61 won't forgive me."

62 Arthur had laid his hand on the soft arm that was nearest to him, and was stooping towards Hetty

63 with a look of coaxing entreaty. Hetty lifted her long dewy lashes, and met the eyes that were bent

64 towards her with a sweet, timid, beseeching look. What a space of time those three moments were

65 while their eyes met and his arms touched her! Love is such a simple thing when we have only one-

66 and-twenty summers and a sweet girl of seventeen trembles under our glance, as if she were a bud

67 first opening her heart with wondering rapture to the morning. Such young unfurrowed souls roll to

68 meet each other like two velvet peaches that touch softly and are at rest; they mingle as easily as two

69 brooklets that ask for nothing but to entwine themselves and ripple with ever-interlacing

70 curves in the leafiest hiding-places. While Arthur gazed into Hetty's dark beseeching eyes, it made no

71 difference to him what sort of English she spoke; and even if hoops and powder had been in fashion,

72 he would very likely not have been sensible just then that Hetty wanted those signs of high breeding.

73 But they started asunder with beating hearts: something had fallen on the ground with a rattling

74 noise; it was Hetty's basket; all her little workwoman's matters were scattered on the path, some of

75 them showing a capability of rolling to great lengths. There was much to be done in picking up, and

76 not a word was spoken; but when Arthur hung the basket over her arm again, the poor child felt a

77 strange difference in his look and manner. He just pressed her hand, and said, with a look and tone

78 that were almost chilling to her, "I have been hindering you; I must not keep you any longer now.

79 You will be expected at the house. Goodbye."

80 Without waiting for her to speak, he turned away from her and hurried back towards the road that led

81 to the Hermitage, leaving Hetty to pursue her way in a strange dream that seemed to have begun in

82 bewildering delight and was now passing into contrarieties and sadness. Would he meet her again as

83 she came home? Why had he spoken almost as if he were displeased with her? And then run away so

84 suddenly? She cried, hardly knowing why.

85 Arthur too was very uneasy, but his feelings were lit up for him by a more distinct consciousness. He

86 hurried to the Hermitage, which stood in the heart of the wood, unlocked the door with a hasty

87 wrench, slammed it after him, pitched Zeluco into the most distant corner, and thrusting his right

88 hand into his pocket, first walked four or five times up and down the scanty length of the little room,

89 and then seated himself on the ottoman in an uncomfortable stiff way, as we often do when we

90 wish not to abandon ourselves to feeling.

91 He was getting in love with Hetty—that was quite plain. He was ready to pitch everything else—no

92 matter where—for the sake of surrendering himself to this delicious feeling which had just disclosed
93 itself. It was no use blinking the fact now—they would get too fond of each other, if he went on
94 taking notice of her—and what would come of it? He should have to go away in a few weeks, and
95 the poor little thing would be miserable. He must not see her alone again; he must keep out of her
96 way. What a fool he was for coming back from Gawaine's!
97 He got up and threw open the windows, to let in the soft breath of the afternoon, and the healthy
98 scent of the firs that made a belt round the Hermitage. The soft air did not help his resolution, as he
99 leaned out and looked into the leafy distance. But he considered his resolution sufficiently fixed:
100 there was no need to debate with himself any longer. He had made up his mind not to meet Hetty
101 again; and now he might give himself up to thinking how immensely agreeable it would be if
102 circumstances were different—how pleasant it would have been to meet her this evening as she
103 came back, and put his arm round her again and look into her sweet face. He wondered if the dear
104 little thing were thinking of him too—twenty to one she was. How beautiful her eyes were with the
105 tear on their lashes! He would like to satisfy his soul for a day with looking at them, and he must see
106 her again—he must see her, simply to remove any false impression from her mind about his manner
107 to her just now. He would behave in a quiet, kind way to her—just to prevent her from going home
108 with her head full of wrong fancies. Yes, that would be the best thing to do after all.
109 It was a long while—more than an hour before Arthur had brought his meditations to this point; but
110 once arrived there, he could stay no longer at the Hermitage. The time must be filled up with
111 movement until he should see Hetty again. And it was already late enough to go and dress for
112 dinner, for his grandfather's dinner-hour was six.

Section One – Comprehension

Spend about 30 minutes on this section

1. How old is Hetty? (Tick **ONE** box) A. Seventeen.. ☐ B. Twenty... ☐ C. Twenty-one.. ☐ D. Nineteen... ☐	1 mark
2. What detail gives the first part of the passage a romantic feel? Lines 1 – 5 (Tick **ONE** box) A. It is afternoon... ☐ B. There are trees covering the path........................... ☐ C. The way destiny is described................................... ☐ D. The way the light filters through the trees.............. ☐	1 mark
3. Which of the following best describes Arthur in lines 1 – 8? (Tick **THREE** boxes) A. Hopeful... ☐ B. Casual.. ☐ C. Fearful.. ☐ D. Happy... ☐ E. Devoted.. ☐ F. Inconsiderate... ☐	3 marks
4. Which four words/phrases suggest nervous in lines 8 – 18? (Tick **FOUR** boxes) A. Ah!... ☐ B. Blushing.. ☐ C. Deep... ☐ D. Fluttered .... ☐	4 marks

33

E. Smiling.. ☐

F. Timid.. ☐

G. Almost frightened.. ☐

---

5. (a) In lines 7 – 12 find a SIMILE. Write out the simile.   1 mark

....

....

(b) Explain the meaning of this simile.

....

....   2 marks

---

6. Look at lines 19 – 28. How do we know Hetty is feeling happy?   1 mark

(Tick **ONE** box)

A. She smiles.. ☐

B. Arthur can't look at her.. ☐

C. She describes feeling as though she is walking on air.................. ☐

D. She feels the same as Arthur.................................... ☐

---

7. What signs are there that Hetty is of a lower class than Arthur in lines   3 marks

29 – 54?

(Tick **THREE** boxes)

A. She is wearing poor clothes..................................... ☐

B. She doesn't know the way to the Hermitage.......................... ☐

C. She is nervous at speaking to someone like Arthur.................... ☐

D. She has intentions of going into service.............................. ☐

E. She is afraid that she will seem stupid to Arthur...................... ☐

F. She is expected home at a certain time............................... ☐

---

8. Based on the passage, which THREE of the following are reasons Hetty   3 marks

gets upset when Arthur mentions Craig, the gardener?

(Tick **THREE** boxes)

A. She is worried what Craig will think if she is talking to Arthur...... ☐

B. She doesn't want Arthur to think she has any affection for Craig... ☐

C. She is angry at Arthur for walking with her......................... ☐ D. She is frustrated that anyone would think she likes Craig............ ☐ E. Her real affections lie with Arthur.................................... ☐ F. She has been traumatised by something Craig has done.............. ☐	
9. Which two words/phrases from lines 58 – 65 suggest that Arthur is a kind man? (Tick **TWO** boxes) A. Gentle voice.. ☐ B. Little blossom.. ☐ C. Beseeching... ☐ D. Come, don't cry... ☐	2 marks
10. Which of the following best describe the emotions Arthur and Hetty have to their encounter from lines 62 to 72? (Tick **TWO** boxes) A. Fixated.. ☐ B. Absurd.. ☐ C. Composed.. ☐ D. Odium... ☐ E. Adoration... ☐ F. Resigned.. ☐	2 marks
11. Why does Arthur suddenly leave?	1 mark
12. Select from the passage one word which most closely corresponds to the word or phrase on the left. The right-hand column below provides guidance regarding which lines to look at to find the correct word. Word from passage Look in lines A. Indolently .... 1 – 5 B. Confines .... 2 – 7 C. Ambiguity .... 20 – 25 D. Misgivings .... 25 – 30	12 marks

E. Shakily	.... 35 – 40	
F. Mortified	.... 55 – 60	
G. Imploring	.... 62 – 65	
H. Apart	.... 70 – 75	
I. Follow	.... 80 – 85	
J. Inadequate	.... 85 – 90	
K. Pledge	.... 95 – 100	
L. Ruminations	.... 105 – 110	

13. What do the questions in lines 82 – 84 show about how Hetty is feeling? Answer in a complete sentence.	1 mark

14. Which THREE of the following best describe the different emotions Arthur feels from lines 84 to the end of the passage? (Tick **THREE** boxes). A. Conflicted.. ☐ B. Miserable.. ☐ C. Resolved.. ☐ D. Confident... ☐ E. Lenient.. ☐ F. Restless... ☐	3 marks

Section Two – Applied Reasoning

Spend about 10 minutes on this section

In the following questions the word in the middle of the second group is made in the same way as the word in the middle of the first group. Complete the second word.

Example:

    (croak   [cash]   shoe)

    (male   [____]   angry)   Answer: mean

Question 1   1 mark

    grab(blog)polo   hale(   )scan

Question 2   1 mark

    came(clap)lope   dose(   )ripe

In the following questions find the two words (one from each group) that are closest in meaning. Underline one word from each group.

Example:

    (boring <u>standard</u> special)   (<u>normal</u> different nice)

Question 3   1 mark

    (smite smoke plume)   (boulder smolder ignite)

Question 4   1 mark

    (gorge feast banquet)   (canyon cannon dynamo)

Question 5   1 mark

Shorter words can be made by rearranging the letters of the word

describe

For example: the word **crib** can be made with four of the letters.

Find five other four-letter words that can be made from 'describe'.

    1. ....

    2. ....

    3. ....

    4. ....

    5. ....

Section Three –
Continuous Writing

Spend about 20 minutes on these 2 questions

1. Write five or six sentences describing your family. Make your writing as vivid as possible. | 15 marks

....

....

....

....

....

....

....

....

2. Write five or six sentences explaining the water cycle. Make your writing as precise as possible.

....

....

....

....

....

....

....

....

End of Test

End of Test

English Mock Exam Paper 2
ANSWERS

Question	Answer	Mark
1.	A	1
2.	D	1
3.	A B D	3
4.	B D F G	4
5.	(a) like a tropic bird among the boughs (b) It shows how she is a flash of colour being glimpsed down the path. *Or similar answer.*	1 1 for idea of colour, 1 for idea of glimpsing
6.	C	1
7.	C D E	3
8.	B D E	3
9.	A D	2
10.	A E	2
11.	He does not want Hetty to get too attached because she will be upset when he has to leave. *Or similar answer.*	1
12.	A. Languidly B. Encloses C. Contradiction D. Scruples E. Tremulously F. Ashamed G. Beseeching H. Asunder I. Pursue J. Scanty K. Resolution L. Meditations	1 1 1 1 1 1 1 1 1 1 1 1

13.	Hetty feels confused as she doesn't understand why Arthur left so suddenly. *Or similar answer, must be in a complete sentence.*	1
14.	A C F	3 marks
Applied Reasoning: Q1: each Q2: drop Q3: smoke, smolder Q4: gorge canyon Q5: bird, reed, ride ribs, dire, beds, seed, seer, bids – there are more, mark any real word as correct. (1 mark for each question)		5 marks
Continuous Writing: This will be marked as one piece of work and the candidate will be assessed on accuracy, spelling, punctuation, the quality of writing and originality.		15 marks
	Total	60 marks

English Mock Exam
Paper 3

Please Complete Your Details:

Name: ....

School: ....

Boy or Girl: ....

Date of Birth: ....

Today's Date: ....

Read the following instructions carefully:

1. Do not open or turn over this page until you have been instructed to do so.

2. Read the text carefully when you are told to do so and then complete the questions that follow.

3. Work as quickly and as carefully as you can.

4. Write your answer to the question ONLY in the space provided.

5. If you want to change your answer, either rub out your original answer or put a single line through it and then write the new answer.

6. If you cannot answer a question, go on to the next question.

7. The number of marks available for each question is indicated in the right-hand margin.

8. Punctuation should be both clear and exact.

9. Where you are asked to choose between a number of possible responses, always choose the **most appropriate** response.

10. You will have **10 minutes** reading time before starting the test.

11. You will have **60 minutes** in total to complete the test.

12. Once the test has begun, you should not ask about questions in the test.

13. When you have completed this practice paper go back to any questions you have missed out and check all of your answers.

English Mock Exam
Paper 3

10 minutes reading time

60 minutes to complete the test

Suggested timing for candidates:

Reading time	10 minutes
Section One – Comprehension	30 minutes
Section Two – Applied Reasoning	10 minutes
Section Three – Continuous Writing	20 minutes

When you are told to do so, carefully read the passage on the next page. After 10 minutes has ended you will have 60 minutes to complete the test. Answer the questions which are on the following pages.

The following passage is from *Agnes Grey* by Anne Brontë

1 We often pity the poor, because they have no leisure to mourn their departed relatives, and
2 necessity obliges them to labour through their severest afflictions: but is not active employment the
3 best remedy for overwhelming sorrow – the surest antidote for despair? It may be a rough
4 comforter: it may seem hard to be harassed with the cares of life when we have no relish for its
5 enjoyments; to be goaded to labour when the heart is ready to break, and the vexed spirit implores
6 for rest only to weep in silence: but is not labour better than the rest we covet? And are not those
7 petty, tormenting cares less hurtful than a continual brooding over the great affliction that
8 oppresses us? Besides, we cannot have cares, and anxieties, and toil, without hope – if it be but the
9 hope of fulfilling our joyless task, accomplishing some needful project, or escaping some further
10 annoyance. At any rate, I was glad my mother had so much employment for every faculty of her
11 action-loving frame. Our kind neighbours lamented that she, once so exalted in wealth and station,
12 should be reduced to such extremity in her time of sorrow; but I am persuaded that she would have
13 suffered thrice as much had she been left in affluence, with liberty to remain in that house, the
14 scene of her early happiness and late affliction, and no stern necessity to prevent her from
15 incessantly brooding over and lamenting her bereavement.
16 I will not dilate upon the feelings with which I left the old house, the well-known garden, the little
17 village church – then doubly dear to me, because my father, who, for thirty years, had taught and
18 prayed within its walls, lay slumbering now beneath its flags – and the old bare hills, delightful in
19 their very desolation, with the narrow vales between, smiling in green wood and sparkling water –
20 the house where I was born, the scene of all my early associations, the place where throughout life
21 my earthly affections had been centred; – and left them to return no more! True, I was going back to
22 Horton Lodge, where, amid many evils, one source of pleasure yet remained: but it was pleasure
23 mingled with excessive pain; and my stay, alas! was limited to six weeks. And even of that precious
24 time, day after day slipped by and I did not see him: except at church, I never saw him for a fortnight
25 after my return. It seemed a long time to me: and, as I was often out with my rambling pupil, of
26 course hopes would keep rising, and disappointments would ensue; and then, I would say to my own
27 heart, 'Here is a convincing proof – if you would but have the sense to see it, or the candour to
28 acknowledge it – that he does not care for you. If he only thought *half* as much about you as you do
29 about him, he would have contrived to meet you many times ere this: you must know that, by
30 consulting your own feelings. Therefore, have done with this nonsense: you have no ground for
31 hope: dismiss, at once, these hurtful thoughts and foolish wishes from your mind, and turn to your
32 own duty, and the dull blank life that lies before you. You might have known such happiness was not
33 for you.'
34 But I saw him at last. He came suddenly upon me as I was crossing a field in returning from a visit to
35 Nancy Brown, which I had taken the opportunity of paying while Matilda Murray was riding her
36 matchless mare. He must have heard of the heavy loss I had sustained: he expressed no sympathy,
37 offered no condolence: but almost the first words he uttered were, – 'How is your mother?' And this
38 was no matter-of-course question, for I never told him that I had a mother: he must have learned
39 the fact from others, if he knew it at all; and, besides, there was sincere goodwill, and even deep,
40 touching, unobtrusive sympathy in the tone and manner of the inquiry. I thanked him with due
41 civility, and told him she was as well as could be expected. 'What will she do?' was the next question.
42 Many would have deemed it an impertinent one, and given an evasive reply; but such an idea never
43 entered my head, and I gave a brief but plain statement of my mother's plans and prospects.

44 'Then you will leave this place shortly?' said he.

45 'Yes, in a month.'

46 He paused a minute, as if in thought. When he spoke again, I hoped it would be to express his

47 concern at my departure; but it was only to say, – 'I should think you will be willing enough to go?'

48 'Yes – for some things,' I replied.

49 'For *some* things only – I wonder what should make you regret it?'

50 I was annoyed at this in some degree; because it embarrassed me: I had only one reason for

51 regretting it; and that was a profound secret, which he had no business to trouble me about.

52 'Why,' said I – 'why should you suppose that I dislike the place?'

53 'You told me so yourself,' was the decisive reply. 'You said, at least, that you could not live

54 contentedly, without a friend; and that you had no friend here, and no possibility of making one –

55 and, besides, I know you must dislike it.'

56 'But if you remember rightly, I said, or meant to say, I could not live contentedly without a friend in

57 the world: I was not so unreasonable as to require one always near me. I think I could be happy in a

58 house full of enemies, if – ' but no; that sentence must not be continued – I paused, and hastily

59 added, – 'And, besides, we cannot well leave a place where we have lived for two or three years,

60 without some feeling of regret.'

61 'Will you regret to part with Miss Murray, your sole remaining pupil and companion?'

62 'I dare say I shall in some degree: it was not without sorrow I parted with her sister.'

63 'I can imagine that.'

64 'Well, Miss Matilda is quite as good – better in one respect.'

65 'What is that?'

66 'She's honest.'

67 'And the other is not?'

68 'I should not call her dishonest; but it must be confessed she's a little artful.'

69 'Artful is she? – I saw she was giddy and vain – and now,' he added, after a pause, 'I can well believe

70 she was artful too; but so excessively so as to assume an aspect of extreme simplicity and unguarded

71 openness. Yes,' continued he, musingly, 'that accounts for some little things that puzzled me a trifle

72 before.'

73 After that, he turned the conversation to more general subjects. He did not leave me till we had

74 nearly reached the park gates: he had certainly stepped a little out of his way to accompany me so

75 far, for he now went back and disappeared down Moss Lane, the entrance of which we had passed

76 some time before. Assuredly I did not regret this circumstance: if sorrow had any place in my heart,

77 it was that he was gone at last – that he was no longer walking by my side, and that that short

78 interval of delightful intercourse was at an end. He had not breathed a word of love, or dropped one

79 hint of tenderness or affection, and yet I had been supremely happy. To be near him, to hear him

80 talk as he did talk, and to feel that he thought me worthy to be so spoken to – capable of

81 understanding and duly appreciating such discourse – was enough.

82 'Yes, Edward Weston, I could indeed be happy in a house full of enemies, if I had but one friend, who

83 truly, deeply, and faithfully loved me; and if that friend were you – though we might be far apart –

84 seldom to hear from each other, still more seldom to meet – though toil, and trouble, and vexation

85 might surround me, still – it would be too much happiness for me to dream of! Yet who can tell,' said

86 I within myself, as I proceeded up the park, – 'who can tell what this one month may bring forth? I

87 have lived nearly three-and-twenty years, and I have suffered much, and tasted little pleasure yet; is

88 it likely my life all through will be so clouded? Is it not possible that God may hear my prayers,

89 disperse these gloomy shadows, and grant me some beams of heaven's sunshine yet? Will He

90 entirely deny to me those blessings which are so freely given to others, who neither ask them nor

91 acknowledge them when received? May I not still hope and trust?' I did hope and trust for a while:

92 but, alas, alas! the time ebbed away: one week followed another, and, excepting one distant glimpse
93 and two transient meetings – during which scarcely anything was said – while I was walking with Miss
94 Matilda, I saw nothing of him: except, of course, at church.

Section One – Comprehension

Spend about 30 minutes on this section

1. What has happened to the narrator's father? (Tick **ONE** box) A. He has been sent to debtor's prison.......................................☐ B. He has had to go to war..☐ C. He has died...☐ D. He has left them for the New World...................................☐	1 mark
2. What is the narrator suggesting is helpful about the way the poor have to deal with mourning? Lines 1 – 12 (Tick **ONE** box) A. They have less feelings than the rich so do not hurt as much.........☐ B. They must work and being kept busy helps deal with the pain.......☐ C. They are able to rest and contemplate their pain......................☐ D. They are usually angry at those who have left and this helps........☐	1 mark
3. Which of the following best describes the narrator in lines 1 – 15? (Tick **THREE** boxes) A. Practical..☐ B. Casual...☐ C. Timid..☐ D. Thankful..☐ E. Passionate..☐ F. Pragmatic...☐	3 marks
4. Which four words/phrases suggest nostalgia in lines 16 – 33? (Tick **FOUR** boxes) A. Dilate...☐ B. Doubly dear..☐ C. Feelings...☐ D. Well-known garden..☐	4 marks

E. Scene of all my early associations.. ☐ F. Lay slumbering.. ☐ G. My earthly affections... ☐	
5. (a) In lines 16 – 19 find an example of PERSONIFICATION. Write it out. .... (b) Explain the meaning of this personification.	1 mark 2 marks
6. How do we know the narrator is feeling conflicted about returning to Horton Lodge? (Tick **ONE** box) A. She describes it as somewhere with both problems as well as joy... ☐ B. She can't wait to return... ☐ C. She wants to leave as soon as she gets there.......................... ☐ D. She feels disappointment at having to return there................... ☐	1 mark
7. Look at lines 23 – 33. What signs are there that the man the narrator wishes to see is not interested in her? (Tick **THREE** boxes) A. He has told her so.. ☐ B. She has seen him with another woman.................................... ☐ C. She has only seen him at church... ☐ D. He is of a higher class than her.. ☐ E. He has not manufactured a reason to see her.......................... ☐ F. He waited two weeks before seeing her at all.......................... ☐	3 marks
8. Which THREE of the following are reasons we could call the narrator pessimistic? (Tick **THREE** boxes) A. She believes she is not destined for joy................................. ☐ B. She is determined to make things right................................... ☐	3 marks

C. She looks for the worst possible reason why Edward hasn't come to see her.. ☐ D. She is not used to any happiness................................. ☐ E. She makes practical use of her time............................. ☐ F. She demands nothing.. ☐	
9. Which two words/phrases from lines 34 – 43 suggest that Edward might care for the narrator? (Tick **TWO** boxes) A. Sincere goodwill... ☐ B. Due civility.. ☐ C. Deep, touching... sympathy...................................... ☐ D. Heavy loss... ☐	2 marks
10. Why would Edward think that the narrator would be glad to leave her place of work? (Tick **TWO** boxes) A. She must want to get away from him............................ ☐ B. He believes she dislikes it there.............................. ☐ C. He knows that she cannot live without a friend and she has no friends there.. ☐ D. It is a place full of misery.................................. ☐ E. It has a reputation of treating people poorly.................. ☐ F. The people she works for are dishonest........................ ☐	2 marks
11. How does the narrator really feel about leaving her place of work?	1 mark
12. Select from the passage one word which most closely corresponds to the word or phrase on the left. The right-hand column below provides guidance regarding which lines to look at to find the correct word.	12 marks

	Word from passage	Look in lines
A. Compels	....	1 – 5
B. Provoked	....	2 – 7
C. Lofty	....	10 – 15

D. Constantly	....	10 – 15
E. Extreme	....	20 – 25
F. Imprudent	....	30 – 35
G. Modest	....	40 – 45
H. Certain	....	50 – 55
I. Thoughtfully	....	70 – 75
J. Definitely	....	75 – 80
K. Displeasure	....	80 – 85
L. Diffuse	....	85 – 90

13. What is the narrator left feeling at the end of the passage? Why? Answer in a complete sentence.	1 mark
14. Write down THREE words or phrases that show this was written over a hundred years ago? A. .... B. .... C.	3 marks

Section Two – Applied Reasoning

Spend about 10 minutes on this section

In the following questions the word in capitals has had three letters next to each other taken out. Find the three letters and put them back into the word without changing their order. The sentence that you make must make sense. *Example:* He was ALS well behaved. Answer: WAY	
Question 1 The staff all wore UNIMS at work. Answer:_____	1 mark
Question 2 The teacher SHED at the naughty children. Answer:	1 mark
In the following questions find one word from each group that will complete the sentence in the best way. Underline the correct answers. *Example:* Kid is to (child <u>goat</u> glove) as foal is to (donkey <u>horse</u> blanket)	
Question 3 wood is to (larch turn wooden) as glass is to (blow floor lasso)	1 mark
Question 4 mile is to (mill yard garden) as kilometre is to (weight metre distance)	1 mark
Question 5 Shorter words can be made by rearranging the letters of the word **bearing** For example: the word **bear** can be made with four of the letters. **Find five other four-letter words that can be made from 'bearing'.** 1. .... 2. .... 3. .... 4. .... 5.	1 mark

Section Three –
Continuous Writing

Spend about 20 minutes on these 2 questions

1. Write five or six sentences describing your favourite place. Make your writing as vivid as possible.	15 marks

....

....

....

....

....

....

....

....

....

2. Write five or six sentences informing people of interesting things to do in your home town. Make your writing as precise as possible.

....

....

....

....

....

....

....

....

....

End of Test

End of Text

English Mock Exam Paper 3
ANSWERS

Question	Answer	Mark
1.	C	1
2.	B	1
3.	A D F	3
4.	B D E G	4
5.	(a) the old bare hills, delightful in their desolation (b) It shows how the narrator likes how lonely and isolated the hills are. *Or similar answer.*	1 1 for idea of liking, 1 for idea of loneliness or isolation
6.	A	1
7.	C E F	3
8.	A C D	3
9.	A C	2
10.	B C	2
11.	She will have regrets as she has been there so long and she will no longer be near Edward. *Or similar answer.*	1
12.	A. Obliges	1
	B. Goaded	1
	C. Exalted	1
	D. Incessantly	1
	E. Excessive	1
	F. Foolish	1
	G. Unobtrusive	1
	H. Decisive	1
	I. Musingly	1
	J. Assuredly	1
	K. Vexation	1
	L. Disperse	1

13.	Disappointment because Edward makes no effort to see and talk to her. *Or similar answer, must be in a complete sentence.*	1
14.	Any of the following: She says 'Alas!' They are all religious. They speak to each other in a formal way. Or any reasonable answer – 1 mark for each correct.	3 marks
Applied Reasoning: Q1: FOR Q2: OUT Q3: turn, blow Q4: yard, metre Q5: bare, ring, grin, near, bang, grab, bean, earn, barn – there are more, mark any real word as correct. (1 mark for each question)		5 marks
Continuous Writing: This will be marked as one piece of work and the candidate will be assessed on accuracy, spelling, punctuation, the quality of writing and originality.		15 marks
	Total	60 marks

English Mock Exam
Paper 4

Please Complete Your Details:

Name: ....

School: ....

Boy or Girl: ....

Date of Birth: ....

Today's Date: ....

Please Complete Your Details:

Name ....

School ....

Boy or Girl: ....

D of Birth: ....

Today's Date: ....

Read the following instructions carefully:

1. Do not open or turn over this page until you have been instructed to do so.

2. Read the text carefully when you are told to do so and then complete the questions that follow.

3. Work as quickly and as carefully as you can.

4. Write your answer to the question ONLY in the space provided.

5. If you want to change your answer, either rub out your original answer or put a single line through it and then write the new answer.

6. If you cannot answer a question, go on to the next question.

7. The number of marks available for each question is indicated in the right-hand margin.

8. Punctuation should be both clear and exact.

9. Where you are asked to choose between a number of possible responses, always choose the **most appropriate** response.

10. You will have **10 minutes** reading time before starting the test.

11. You will have **60 minutes** in total to complete the test.

12. Once the test has begun, you should not ask about questions in the test.

13. When you have completed this practice paper go back to any questions you have missed out and check all of your answers.

English Mock Exam
Paper 4

10 minutes reading time
60 minutes to complete the test

Suggested timing for candidates:

Reading time	10 minutes
Section One – Comprehension	30 minutes
Section Two – Applied Reasoning	10 minutes
Section Three – Continuous Writing	20 minutes

When you are told to do so, carefully read the passage on the next page. After 10 minutes has ended you will have 60 minutes to complete the test. Answer the questions which are on the following pages.

The following passage is from *The Aspern Papers* by Henry James

1 It was certainly strange beyond all strangeness, and I shall not take up space with attempting to explain it that
2 whereas in all these other lines of research we had to deal with phantoms and dust, the mere echoes of
3 echoes, the one living source of information that had lingered on into our time had been unheeded by us.
4 Every one of Aspern's contemporaries had, according to our belief, passed away; we had not been able to look
5 into a single pair of eyes into which his had looked or to feel a transmitted contact in any aged hand that his
6 had touched. Most dead of all did poor Miss Bordereau appear, and yet she alone had survived. We exhausted
7 in the course of months our wonder that we had not found her out sooner, and the substance of our
8 explanation was that she had kept so quiet. The poor lady on the whole had had reason for doing so. But it
9 was a revelation to us that it was possible to keep so quiet as that in the latter half of the nineteenth century
10 —the age of newspapers and telegrams and photographs and interviewers. And she had taken no great
11 trouble about it either: she had not hidden herself away in an undiscoverable hole; she had boldly settled
12 down in a city of exhibition. The only secret of her safety that we could perceive was that Venice contained so
13 many curiosities that were greater than she. And then accident had somehow favoured her, as was shown for
14 example in the fact that Mrs Prest had never happened to mention her to me, though I had spent three weeks
15 in Venice—under her nose, as it were—five years before. Mrs Prest had not mentioned this much to anyone;
16 she appeared almost to have forgotten she was there. Of course she had not the responsibilities of an editor.
17 It was no explanation of the old woman's having eluded us to say that she lived abroad, for our researches had
18 again and again taken us (not only by correspondence but by personal inquiry) to France, to Germany, to Italy,
19 in which countries, not counting his important stay in England, so many of the too few years of Aspern's career
20 were spent. We were glad to think at least that in all our publishings (some people consider I believe that we
21 have overdone them), we had only touched in passing and in the most discreet manner on Miss Bordereau's
22 connection. Oddly enough, even if we had had the material (and we often wondered what had become of it),
23 it would have been the most difficult episode to handle.
24 The gondola stopped, the old palace was there; it was a house of the class which in Venice carries even in
25 extreme dilapidation the dignified name. "How charming! It's grey and pink!" my companion exclaimed; and
26 that is the most comprehensive description of it. It was not particularly old, only two or three centuries; and it
27 had an air not so much of decay as of quiet discouragement, as if it had rather missed its career. But its wide
28 front, with a stone balcony from end to end of the piano nobile or most important floor, was architectural
29 enough, with the aid of various pilasters and arches; and the stucco with which in the intervals it had long ago
30 been endued was rosy in the April afternoon. It overlooked a clean, melancholy, unfrequented canal, which
31 had a narrow riva or convenient footway on either side. "I don't know why there are no brick gables," said
32 Mrs Prest, "but this corner has seemed to me before more Dutch than Italian, more like Amsterdam than like
33 Venice. It's perversely clean, for reasons of its own; and though you can pass on foot scarcely anyone ever
34 thinks of doing so. It has the air of a Protestant Sunday. Perhaps the people are afraid of the Misses
35 Bordereau. I daresay they have the reputation of witches."
36 I forget what answer I made to this—I was given up to two other reflections. The first of these was that if the
37 old lady lived in such a big, imposing house she could not be in any sort of misery and therefore would not be
38 tempted by a chance to let a couple of rooms. I expressed this idea to Mrs Prest, who gave me a very logical
39 reply. "If she didn't live in a big house how could it be a question of her having rooms to spare? If she were not
40 amply lodged herself you would lack ground to approach her. Besides, a big house here, and especially in this
41 quartier perdu, proves nothing at all: it is perfectly compatible with a state of penury. Dilapidated old palazzi,
42 if you will go out of the way for them, are to be had for five shillings a year. And as for the people who live in
43 them—no, until you have explored Venice socially as much as I have you can form no idea of their domestic

44 desolation. They live on nothing, for they have nothing to live on." The other idea that had come into my head
45 was connected with a high blank wall which appeared to confine an expanse of ground on one side of the
46 house. Blank I call it, but it was figured over with the patches that please a painter, repaired breaches,
47 crumblings of plaster, extrusions of brick that had turned pink with time; and a few thin trees, with the poles
48 of certain rickety trellises, were visible over the top. The place was a garden, and apparently it belonged to the
49 house. It suddenly occurred to me that if it did belong to the house I had my pretext.
50 I sat looking out on all this with Mrs Prest (it was covered with the golden glow of Venice) from the shade of
51 our felze, and she asked me if I would go in then, while she waited for me, or come back another time. At first
52 I could not decide—it was doubtless very weak of me. I wanted still to think I might get a footing, and I was
53 afraid to meet failure, for it would leave me, as I remarked to my companion, without another arrow for my
54 bow. "Why not another?" she inquired as I sat there hesitating and thinking it over; and she wished to know
55 why even now and before taking the trouble of becoming an inmate (which might be wretchedly
56 uncomfortable after all, even if it succeeded), I had not the resource of simply offering them a sum of money
57 down. In that way I might obtain the documents without bad nights.
58 "Dearest lady," I exclaimed, "excuse the impatience of my tone when I suggest that you must have forgotten
59 the very fact (surely I communicated it to you) which pushed me to throw myself upon your ingenuity. The old
60 woman won't have the documents spoken of; they are personal, delicate, intimate, and she hasn't modern
61 notions, God bless her! If I should sound that note first I should certainly spoil the game. I can arrive at the
62 papers only by putting her off her guard, and I can put her off her guard only by ingratiating diplomatic
63 practices. Hypocrisy, duplicity are my only chance. I am sorry for it, but for Jeffrey Aspern's sake I would do
64 worse still. First I must take tea with her; then tackle the main job." And I told over what had happened to
65 John Cumnor when he wrote to her. No notice whatever had been taken of his first letter, and the second had
66 been answered very sharply, in six lines, by the niece. "Miss Bordereau requested her to say that she could not
67 imagine what he meant by troubling them. They had none of Mr. Aspern's papers, and if they had should
68 never think of showing them to anyone on any account whatever. She didn't know what he was talking about
69 and begged he would let her alone." I certainly did not want to be met that way.
70 "Well," said Mrs Prest after a moment, provokingly, "perhaps after all they haven't any of his things. If they
71 deny it flat how are you sure?"
72 "John Cumnor is sure, and it would take me long to tell you how his conviction, or his very strong presumption
73 —strong enough to stand against the old lady's not unnatural fib—has built itself up. Besides, he makes much
74 of the internal evidence of the niece's letter."
75 "The internal evidence?"
76 "Her calling him 'Mr Aspern.'"
77 "I don't see what that proves."
78 "It proves familiarity, and familiarity implies the possession of mementoes, or relics. I can't tell you how that
79 'Mr' touches me—how it bridges over the gulf of time and brings our hero near to me—nor what an edge it
80 gives to my desire to see Juliana. You don't say, 'Mr.' Shakespeare."
81 "Would I, any more, if I had a box full of his letters?"
82 "Yes, if he had been your lover and someone wanted them!" And I added that John Cumnor was so convinced,
83 and so all the more convinced by Miss Bordereau's tone, that he would have come himself to Venice on the
84 business were it not that for him there was the obstacle that it would be difficult to disprove his identity with
85 the person who had written to them, which the old ladies would be sure to suspect in spite of dissimulation
86 and a change of name. If they were to ask him point-blank if he were not their correspondent it would be too
87 awkward for him to lie; whereas I was fortunately not tied in that way. I was a fresh hand and could say no
88 without lying.
89 "But you will have to change your name," said Mrs Prest. "Juliana lives out of the world as much as it is
90 possible to live, but none the less she has probably heard of Mr Aspern's editors; she perhaps possesses what
91 you have published."

92 "I have thought of that," I returned; and I drew out of my pocketbook a visiting card, neatly engraved with a
93 name that was not my own.

94 "You are very extravagant; you might have written it," said my companion.

95 "This looks more genuine."

96 "Certainly, you are prepared to go far! But it will be awkward about your letters; they won't come to you in
97 that mask."

98 "My banker will take them in, and I will go every day to fetch them. It will give me a little walk."

99 "Shall you only depend upon that?" asked Mrs Prest. "Aren't you coming to see me?"

100 "Oh, you will have left Venice, for the hot months, long before there are any results. I am prepared to roast all
101 summer—as well as hereafter, perhaps you'll say! Meanwhile, John Cumnor will bombard me with letters
102 addressed, in my feigned name, to the care of the padrona."

103 "She will recognize his hand," my companion suggested.

104 "On the envelope he can disguise it."

105 "Well, you're a precious pair! Doesn't it occur to you that even if you are able to say you are not Mr Cumnor
106 in person they may still suspect you of being his emissary?"

107 "Certainly, and I see only one way to parry that."

108 "And what may that be?"

109 I hesitated a moment. "To make love to the niece."

110 "Ah," cried Mrs Prest, "wait till you see her!"

Section One – Comprehension

Spend about 30 minutes on this section

1. Where is the story set? (Tick **ONE** box) A. France... ☐ B. Germany.. ☐ C. England.. ☐ D. Venice.. ☐	1 mark
2. Which of the following is true based on the information in lines 1-10? (Tick **ONE** box) A. Aspern was a well-loved person.............................. ☐ B. Aspern has only one friend alive in the world........................ ☐ C. Aspern is a notorious criminal................................. ☐ D. The narrator is a lawyer.................................... ☐	1 mark
3. Which of the following best describes Mrs Prest? (Tick **THREE** boxes) A. Secretive... ☐ B. Forgetful... ☐ C. Confident... ☐ D. Furious... ☐ E. Rational.. ☐ F. Pedantic... ☐	3 marks
4. Which four words/phrases suggest mystery in lines 1 – 15? (Tick **FOUR** boxes) A. Strange.. ☐ B. Attempting to explain it................................. ☐ C. Mere echoes.. ☐ D. Phantoms... ☐	4 marks

E. Transmitted contact... ☐	
F. One living source.. ☐	
G. Not mentioned.. ☐	
5. (a) In lines 1 – 5 find an example of METAPHOR. Write it out. .... (b) Explain the meaning of this metaphor.	1 mark 2 marks
6. What ruse does the narrator plan to use to make contact with Miss Bordereau? (Tick **ONE** box) A. To ask about Aspern....................................... ☐ B. To pretend to be a long lost relative..................... ☐ C. To pretend to be a buildings inspector.................. ☐ D. To pretend to be a lodger looking for a room to rent.............. ☐	1 mark
7. Look at lines 26 – 51. What signs are there that Miss Bordereau is not rich? (Tick **THREE** boxes) A. Her house is not in a very expensive area............... ☐ B. She is looking for lodgers................................. ☐ C. Her house is in a state of disrepair...................... ☐ D. She has a very large house............................... ☐ E. Houses such as hers cost very little..................... ☐ F. She only earns a very little wage......................... ☐	3 marks
8. Which THREE of the following are reasons we could call Mrs Prest Intelligent? (Tick **THREE** boxes) A. She is well educated..................................... ☐ B. She has a good knowledge of the world and architecture............ ☐ C. She gives sound answers to the narrator's questions................. ☐ D. She has an excellent job................................. ☐	3 marks

E. She makes inane remarks... ☐		
F. She is careful to think up possible problems to the narrator's plan... ☐		
9. Which two words/phrases from lines 58 – 71 suggest that the narrator may be patronising towards Mrs Prest? (Tick **TWO** boxes) A. Dearest lady.. ☐ B. Impatience of my tone... ☐ C. Exclaimed... ☐ D. Ingratiating... ☐	2 marks
10. Why does the narrator think that only deception is going to work? (Tick **TWO** boxes) A. Miss Bordereau is a dishonest person herself........................ ☐ B. Previous attempts to be truthful haven't worked...................... ☐ C. She has been too used to being secretive........................... ☐ D. He thinks she needs to be tricked first if he is going to succeed..... ☐ E. She is a well-known con artist....................................... ☐	2 marks
11. How does the narrator know that Miss Bordereau knew Aspern?	1 mark
12. Select from the passage one word which most closely corresponds to the word or phrase on the left. The right-hand column below provides guidance regarding which lines to look at to find the correct word. Word from passage Look in lines A. Meagre .... 1 – 5 B. Distinguish .... 2 – 7 C. Evaded .... 10 – 15 D. Collapse .... 10 – 15 E. Attracted .... 20 – 25 F. Span .... 30 – 35 G. Acquaintance .... 40 – 45	12 marks

H. Obsequious	.... 50 – 55	
I. Suggests	.... 70 – 75	
J. Concealment	.... 75 – 80	
K. Profligate	.... 80 – 85	
L. Contrived	.... 85 – 90	
13. Why would we describe the narrator as devious by the end of the passage? Answer in a complete sentence.	1 mark
14. Write down TWO words or phrases that show this is set in a different country? A. .... B.	3 marks

Section Two – Applied Reasoning

Spend about 10 minutes on this section

A B C D E F G H I J K L M N O P Q R S T U V W X Y Z The above alphabet is there to help you with these questions. Find the letters that complete each question in the best way. *Example:* AB is to CD as PQ is to ( ) Answer: RS	
Question 1 WP is to DK as FS is to (___)	1 mark
Question 2 DM is to LI as WT is to (___)	1 mark
In the following questions find the two words (one from each group) that are most opposite in meaning. Underline one word from each group. *Example:* (<u>up</u> high sky) (side jump <u>down</u>)	
Question 3 (radical radius rebellious) (modern moderate miraculous)	1 mark
Question 4 (compose oppose compassion) (support preside troublesome)	1 mark
Question 5 Shorter words can be made by rearranging the letters of the word **defuse** For example: the word **fuse** can be made with four of the letters. **Find five other four-letter words that can be made from 'defuse'.** 1. .... 2. .... 3.	1 mark

4. ....

5. ....

Section Three – Continuous Writing

Spend about 20 minutes on these 2 questions

1. Write five or six sentences describing the room you are in. Make your writing as vivid as possible.	15 marks

....

....

....

....

....

....

....

....

....

....

2. Write five or six sentences persuading people to visit a theme park of your choice. Make your writing as precise as possible.

....

....

....

....

....

....

....

....

....

....

End of Test

English Mock Exam Paper 4
ANSWERS

Question	Answer	Mark
1.	D	1
2.	B	1
3.	B E F	3
4.	A B C D	4
5.	(a) we had to deal with phantoms and dust (b) It means the narrator was digging into the *past, nothing was alive* for him to *investigate. Or similar answer*	1 1 for idea of past, 1 for idea of nothing being alive OR investigation
6.	D	1
7.	A C E	3
8.	B C F	3
9.	A B	2
10.	B D	2
11.	She addressed him as 'Mr' Aspern in a letter which she wouldn't do if she didn't know him well. *Or similar answer.*	1
12.	A. Mere B. Perceive C. Eluded D. Dilapidation E. Tempted F. Expanse G. Companion H. Ingratiating I. Implies J. Dissimulation K. Extravagant L. Feigned	1 1 1 1 1 1 1 1 1 1 1 1

13.	He is devious because he is trying to trick Miss Bordereau by changing his name and deceiving her as to the real reason he is there. *Or similar answer, must be in a complete sentence.*	1 for idea of tricking or deceiving, 1 for details of such deception
14.	Any of the following: Gondola Palazzi Felze Padrona Or any reasonable answer – 1 mark for each correct.	2 marks
Applied Reasoning: Q1: UH Q2: EP Q3: radical, moderate Q4: oppose, support Q5: seed, used, sued, feed, dues – there are more, mark any real word as correct. (1 mark for each question)		5 marks
Continuous Writing: This will be marked as one piece of work and the candidate will be assessed on accuracy, spelling, punctuation, the quality of writing and originality.		15 marks
	Total	60 marks

English Mock Exam
Paper 5

Please Complete Your Details:

Name: ....

School: ....

Boy or Girl: ....

Date of Birth: ....

Today's Date: ....

Read the following instructions carefully:

1. Do not open or turn over this page until you have been instructed to do so.

2. Read the text carefully when you are told to do so and then complete the questions that follow.

3. Work as quickly and as carefully as you can.

4. Write your answer to the question ONLY in the space provided.

5. If you want to change your answer, either rub out your original answer or put a single line through it and then write the new answer.

6. If you cannot answer a question, go on to the next question.

7. The number of marks available for each question is indicated in the right-hand margin.

8. Punctuation should be both clear and exact.

9. Where you are asked to choose between a number of possible responses, always choose the **most appropriate** response.

10. You will have **10 minutes** reading time before starting the test.

11. You will have **60 minutes** in total to complete the test.

12. Once the test has begun, you should not ask about questions in the test.

13. When you have completed this practice paper go back to any questions you have missed out and check all of your answers.

English Mock Exam Paper 5

10 minutes reading time
60 minutes to complete the test

Suggested timing for candidates:

Reading time	10 minutes
Section One – Comprehension	30 minutes
Section Two – Applied Reasoning	10 minutes
Section Three – Continuous Writing	20 minutes

When you are told to do so, carefully read the passage on the next page. After 10 minutes has ended you will have 60 minutes to complete the test. Answer the questions which are on the following pages.

The following passage is from *The Chimes*
by Charles Dickens

1 Here are not many people - and as it is desirable that a storyteller and a story-reader should

2 establish a mutual understanding as soon as possible, I beg it to be noticed that I confine this

3 observation neither to young people nor to little people, but extend it to all conditions of people:

4 little and big, young and old: yet growing up, or already growing down again - there are not, I say,

5 many people who would care to sleep in a church. I don't mean at sermon-time in warm weather

6 (when the thing has actually been done, once or twice), but in the night, and alone. A great

7 multitude of persons will be violently astonished, I know, by this position, in the broad bold Day. But

8 it applies to Night. It must be argued by night, and I will undertake to maintain it successfully on any

9 gusty winter's night appointed for the purpose, with any one opponent chosen from the rest, who

10 will meet me singly in an old churchyard, before an old church-door; and will previously empower

11 me to lock him in, if needful to his satisfaction, until morning.

12 For the night-wind has a dismal trick of wandering round and round a building of that sort, and

13 moaning as it goes; and of trying, with its unseen hand, the windows and the doors; and seeking out

14 some crevices by which to enter. And when it has got in; as one not finding what it seeks, whatever

15 that may be, it wails and howls to issue forth again: and not content with stalking through the aisles,

16 and gliding round and round the pillars, and tempting the deep organ, soars up to the roof, and

17 strives to rend the rafters: then flings itself despairingly upon the stones below, and passes,

18 muttering, into the vaults. Anon, it comes up stealthily, and creeps along the walls, seeming to read

19 in whispers, the Inscriptions sacred to the Dead. At some of these, it breaks out shrilly, as with

20 laughter; and at others, moans and cries as if it were lamenting. It has a ghostly sound too, lingering

21 within the altar; where it seems to chant, in its wild way, of Wrong and Murder done, and false Gods

22 worshipped, in defiance of the Tables of the Law, which look so fair and smooth, but are so flawed

23 and broken. Ugh! Heaven preserve us, sitting snugly round the fire! It has an awful voice, that wind

24 at Midnight, singing in a church!

25 But, high up in the steeple! There the foul blast roars and whistles! High up in the steeple, where it is

26 free to come and go through many an airy arch and loophole, and to twist and twine itself about the

27 giddy stair, and twirl the groaning weathercock, and make the very tower shake and shiver! High up

28 in the steeple, where the belfry is, and iron rails are ragged with rust, and sheets of lead and copper,

29 shrivelled by the changing weather, crackle and heave beneath the unaccustomed tread; and birds

30 stuff shabby nests into corners of old oaken joists and beams; and dust grows old and grey; and

31 speckled spiders, indolent and fat with long security, swing idly to and fro in the vibration of the

32 bells, and never loose their hold upon their thread-spun castles in the air, or climb up sailor-like in

33 quick alarm, or drop upon the ground and ply a score of nimble legs to save one life! High up in the

34 steeple of an old church, far above the light and murmur of the town and far below the flying clouds

35 that shadow it, is the wild and dreary place at night: and high up in the steeple of an old church,

36 dwelt the Chimes I tell of.

37 They were old Chimes, trust me. Centuries ago, these Bells had been baptized by bishops: so many

38 centuries ago, that the register of their baptism was lost long, long before the memory of man, and

39 no one knew their names. They had had their Godfathers and Godmothers, these Bells (for my own

40 part, by the way, I would rather incur the responsibility of being Godfather to a Bell than a Boy), and

41 had their silver mugs no doubt, besides. But Time had mowed down their sponsors, and Henry the

42 Eighth had melted down their mugs; and they now hung, nameless and mugless, in the church-

43 tower.

44 Not speechless, though. Far from it. They had clear, loud, lusty sounding voices, had these Bells; and
45 far and wide they might be heard upon the wind. Much too sturdy Chimes were they, to be
46 dependent on the pleasure of the wind, moreover; for, fighting gallantly against it when it took an
47 adverse whim, they would pour their cheerful notes into a listening ear right royally; and bent on
48 being heard on stormy nights, by some poor mother watching a sick child, or some lone wife whose
49 husband was at sea, they had been sometimes known to beat a blustering Nor' Wester; aye, 'all to
50 fits,' as Toby Veck said; - for though they chose to call him Trotty Veck, his name was Toby, and
51 nobody could make it anything else either (except Tobias) without a special act of parliament; he
52 having been as lawfully christened in his day as the Bells had been in theirs, though with not quite so
53 much of solemnity or public rejoicing.
54 For my part, I confess myself of Toby Veck's belief, for I am sure he had opportunities enough of
55 forming a correct one. And whatever Toby Veck said, I say. And I take my stand by Toby Veck,
56 although he did stand all day long (and weary work it was) just outside the church-door. In fact he
57 was a ticket-porter, Toby Veck, and waited there for jobs.
58 And a breezy, goose-skinned, blue-nosed, red-eyed, stony-toed, tooth-chattering place it was, to
59 wait in, in the winter-time, as Toby Veck well knew. The wind came tearing round the corner –
60 especially the east wind—as if it had sallied forth, express, from the confines of the earth, to have a
61 blow at Toby. And oftentimes it seemed to come upon him sooner than it had expected, for
62 bouncing round the corner, and passing Toby, it would suddenly wheel round again, as if it cried
63 'Why, here he is!' Incontinently his little white apron would be caught up over his head like a
64 naughty boy's garments, and his feeble little cane would be seen to wrestle and struggle unavailingly
65 in his hand, and his legs would undergo tremendous agitation, and Toby himself all aslant, and facing
66 now in this direction, now in that, would be so banged and buffeted, and to touzled, and worried,
67 and hustled, and lifted off his feet, as to render it a state of things but one degree removed from a
68 positive miracle, that he wasn't carried up bodily into the air as a colony of frogs or snails or other
69 very portable creatures sometimes are, and rained down again, to the great astonishment of the
70 natives, on some strange corner of the world where ticket-porters are unknown.
71 But, windy weather, in spite of its using him so roughly, was, after all, a sort of holiday for Toby.
72 That's the fact. He didn't seem to wait so long for a sixpence in the wind, as at other times; the
73 having to fight with that boisterous element took off his attention, and quite freshened him up,
74 when he was getting hungry and low-spirited. A hard frost too, or a fall of snow, was an Event; and it
75 seemed to do him good, somehow or other - it would have been hard to say in what respect though,
76 Toby! So wind and frost and snow, and perhaps a good stiff storm of hail, were Toby Veck's red-
77 letter days.
78 Wet weather was the worst; the cold, damp, clammy wet, that wrapped him up like a moist great-
79 coat—the only kind of great-coat Toby owned, or could have added to his comfort by dispensing
80 with. Wet days, when the rain came slowly, thickly, obstinately down; when the street's throat, like
81 his own, was choked with mist; when smoking umbrellas passed and re-passed, spinning round and
82 round like so many teetotums, as they knocked against each other on the crowded footway,
83 throwing off a little whirlpool of uncomfortable sprinklings; when gutters brawled and waterspouts
84 were full and noisy; when the wet from the projecting stones and ledges of the church fell drip, drip,
85 drip, on Toby, making the wisp of straw on which he stood mere mud in no time; those were the
86 days that tried him. Then, indeed, you might see Toby looking anxiously out from his shelter in an
87 angle of the church wall—such a meagre shelter that in summer time it never cast a shadow thicker
88 than a good-sized walking stick upon the sunny pavement—with a disconsolate and lengthened
89 face. But coming out, a minute afterwards, to warm himself by exercise, and trotting up and down
90 some dozen times, he would brighten even then, and go back more brightly to his niche.

Section One – Comprehension

Spend about 30 minutes on this section

1. Who is the protagonist of the story? (Tick **ONE** box) A. The wind.. ☐ B. The church bells.. ☐ C. The narrator... ☐ D. Toby Veck.. ☐	1 mark
2. Which of the following is the correct definition of the narrator? (Tick **ONE** box) A. 3rd person narrator... ☐ B. 1st person narrator... ☐ C. 2nd person narrator.. ☐	1 mark
3. Which of the following best describes the wind in this passage? (Tick **THREE** boxes) A. Relentless... ☐ B. Malicious.. ☐ C. Joyful... ☐ D. Mild... ☐ E. All encompassing... ☐ F. Benevolent... ☐	3 marks
4. Which four words/phrases suggest strength of movement in lines 12 – 36? (Tick **FOUR** boxes) A. Flings itself... ☐ B. Soars up... ☐ C. Twirl.. ☐ D. Stalking through.. ☐ E. Foul blast roars.. ☐ F. Creeps along.. ☐	4 marks

G. It wails and howls... ☐	
5. (a) In lines 12 – 36 what literary device is used to describe the weather? .... (b) Explain the effect of this device.	1 mark 2 marks
6. What does the narrator say has happened to the bells? (Tick **ONE** box) A. They have lost their voices................................ ☐ B. They have been well maintained.......................... ☐ C. They have been neglected over time..................... ☐ D. They have fallen out of the tower........................ ☐	1 mark
7. Which THREE of the following are true about the bells? (Tick **THREE** boxes) A. They are certain they will be used again................. ☐ B. They love to sound out..................................... ☐ C. They give solace to those who hear them................ ☐ D. They have never been wanted.............................. ☐ E. They are a vital part of the community................... ☐ F. There was a time when these bells were named......... ☐	3 marks
8. Which THREE of the following best describe Toby Veck? (Tick **THREE** boxes) A. The narrator respects his opinion......................... ☐ B. Strong... ☐ C. Merciless.. ☐ D. Poor.. ☐ E. Weak... ☐ F. Lenient... ☐	3 marks

9. Which two words/phrases from lines 58 – 70 suggest that the wind is cold? (Tick **TWO** boxes) A. Goose-skinned.. ☐ B. Sallied forth.. ☐ C. Struggle unavailingly....................................... ☐ D. Tooth-chattering... ☐	2 marks
10. Why does Toby see windy weather as a 'sort of holiday'? (Tick **TWO** boxes) A. He doesn't have to struggle for money in the wind................. ☐ B. Hail is better for gaining money........................... ☐ C. Rain and dampness is far worse........................... ☐ D. He gets the day off when it is windy..................... ☐ E. He likes thinking that he has beaten the wind...................... ☐	2 marks
11. In the last paragraph of the passage, what do pedestrians do that make things worse for Toby?	1 mark
12. Select from the passage one word which most closely corresponds to the word or phrase on the left. The right-hand column below provides guidance regarding which lines to look at to find the correct word. <table><tr><td></td><td>Word from passage</td><td>Look in lines</td></tr><tr><td>A. Common</td><td>.............................</td><td>1 – 5</td></tr><tr><td>B. Chosen</td><td>.............................</td><td>5 – 10</td></tr><tr><td>C. Sanction</td><td>.............................</td><td>10 – 15</td></tr><tr><td>D. Furtively</td><td>.............................</td><td>15 – 20</td></tr><tr><td>E. Remaining</td><td>.............................</td><td>20 – 25</td></tr><tr><td>F. Lurch</td><td>.............................</td><td>25 – 30</td></tr><tr><td>G. Lazy</td><td>.............................</td><td>28 – 32</td></tr><tr><td>H. Obligation</td><td>.............................</td><td>36 – 42</td></tr></table>	12 marks

I. Urge	....	45 – 50	
J. Somberness	....	50 – 55	
K. Propelled	....	65 – 70	
L. Stubbornly	....	80 – 85	

13. What is Toby's biggest enemy? Answer in a complete sentence.	2 marks

14. How does the narrator feel about Toby? (Tick **TWO** boxes) A. He hates him.. ☐ B. He likes that he looks on the positive side........................... ☐ C. He has high esteem for him..................................... ☐ D. He thinks he is pathetic.. ☐	2 marks

Section Two – Applied Reasoning

Spend about 10 minutes on this section

In the following questions one letter can be moved from the first word to the second word making two new words. The order of the letters must not be changed and the new words must make sense. *Example:* crane cat Answer: r	
Question 1 pursue cold Answer:_____	1 mark
Question 2 sidle air Answer:_____	1 mark
A B C D E F G H I J K L M N O P Q R S T U V W X Y Z The above alphabet is there to help you with these questions. Find the next letters in the sequence. *Example:* DR EQ FP GO (??) Answer: HN	
Question 3 OD WV EN MF UX (_____)	1 mark
Question 4 PG QH SJ VM ZQ (_____)	1 mark

Question 5
Shorter words can be made by rearranging the letters of the word.
 	
                  stranger
For example: the word **rang** can be made with four of the letters.
 	
Find five other four-letter words that can be made from 'stranger'.
 	
    1. ....
 	
    2. ....
 	
    3. ....
 	
    4. ....
 	
    5. ....
	1 mark

Section Three –
Continuous Writing

Spend about 20 minutes on these 2 questions

1. Write five or six sentences describing a sunny day. Make your writing as vivid as possible.	15 marks

....

....

....

....

....

....

....

....

....

2. Write five or six sentences persuading people to become your best friend. Make your writing as precise as possible.

....

....

....

....

....

....

....

....

End of Test

End of Test

English Mock Exam Paper 5
ANSWERS

Question	Answer	Mark
1.	D	1
2.	A	1
3.	A B E	3
4.	A B E G	4
5.	(a) Personification (b) It makes the wind seem like a person who is able to invade all parts of the church. It makes the wind sound scary. *Or similar answer*	1 1 for idea of the wind being a person, 1 for idea of creating fear
6.	C	1
7.	B C F	3
8.	A D E	3
9.	A D	2
10.	A C	2
11.	Their umbrellas get knocked and cause more water to fall on Toby. *Or similar answer.*	1
12.	A. Mutual B. Appointed C. Empower D. Stealthily E. Lingering F. Heave G. Indolent H. Responsibility I. Whim J. Solemnity K. Hustled L. Obstinately	1 1 1 1 1 1 1 1 1 1 1 1

13.	Weather is Toby's biggest enemy. *Or similar answer, must be in a complete sentence.*	1 for a complete sentence, 1 for weather or rain
14.	B C	2 marks

Applied Reasoning:	5 marks
Q1: U Q2: L Q3: CP Q4: EV Q5: gets, rats, tars, star, gear, near, rant – there are more, mark any real word as correct. (1 mark for each question)	

Continuous Writing:	15 marks
This will be marked as one piece of work and the candidate will be assessed on accuracy, spelling, punctuation, the quality of writing and originality.	

	Total	60 marks

If you wish to further develop your understanding and gain access to additional practice questions then you can sign up to the S6 Hub via www.S6tutoringacademy.co.uk

The S6 Hub is an online educational resource containing a wide variety of questions and practice materials in Maths, English, Verbal Reasoning, Non-Verbal Reasoning, Science and Spanish.

The S6 Hub 'Test Zone' is where students can attempt either individual topic or whole subject tests, with all tests being timed and instantly marked. The hub also offers an array of feedback and benchmarking tools to help you tailor your learning and monitor your progress.

Lightning Source UK Ltd.
Milton Keynes UK
UKOW07f2215220715

255663UK00002B/2/P